AF365748

For Younger Self

- Jayada S. Sarela

For My Family

- Marina Halak

COPYRIGHT © JAYADA S.SARELA

🌐 **www.jayadasarela.com**

Published by: *Vala Sajja*

EBOOK Edition September 2020

Book Design and Illustration by *Marina Halak*

(EBOOK)

ISBN no. **978-616-572-127-1**

MOLi

AND THE

MAGIC TUNNEL

Written by Jayada S. Sarela   Illustrated by Marina Halak

Moli was a curious boy who loved to read.
His curiosity made him do things differently.
Others thought he was odd, so he was often left out alone.

When Moli was little, his grandpa always
brought him into the forest.
" Moli the forest loves you
beyond what your eyes can see."

"It loves your differences.
It loves you when you think you are not good enough.
It loves you as much as when you truly love yourself."

"Sit next to me and close your eyes,
smell the wildflowers,
the grasses, and the leafy trees.
Let them fill up your heart and extend
to every part of your body."

Whenever Moli felt lonely
and missed his grandpa,
he would go into the forest,
close his eyes, smell the forest
air and feel the love and
his grandpa's presence.

One evening as he was left out alone, he wandered off into the forest.
There were beautiful wildflowers surrounding the entrance of a tunnel.
Moli was curious so he explored farther and farther as the tunnel grew
 darker and darker.
 " Hello!", a voice echoed in the tunnel,
" I am Tubee, a time machine tunnel..I have been waiting for you!"

Soon enough, they became best friends.

" Moli, use this magic wand and draw it around yourself
followed by three long breaths.
This is how you call me for a journey to the past!"

" Let's go back to the past to see my grandpa!
I miss him Tubee!"

Moli felt his feet firmly on the ground and
drew around himself. Breathing in slowly,
feeling cool air enter his nose, he grew
bigger and bigger. Then, breathing out
slowly, he got smaller and smaller..

One time...

Two times...

Three times...

Moli found himself in the place where his grandpa had lived a long time ago.
" Wow grandpa is so young and strong! Others think he looks different
but he seems to love being different!"
Everyone liked and admired him and his smile was always there.

" Tubee, I can see everything changes with time,
but is there anything else I cannot see that changes too?"

" Of course, but I can't show you that Moli!, you have to feel them.."
" Feelings?.." Tubee said.

" Ah, I have an idea!"
Everyday before sunset, Moli would sit by
the river sketching his reflections.

" Wow, I look like a monster when I am angry!
I breathe so fast!!"

" Oh..today, I feel bored.
My body has no energy!"

"So sad..I feel like crying today!"

Moli was curious if he could control what he wished to feel each day; he realized he couldn't!
He tried to avoid feeling sadness by keeping himself busy, but sadness came right back when he was about to sleep.

THURSDAY
FRIDAY
SUNDAY
HURSDAY
SA TARDAY
U
SA TURDAY
EDNESD
AY
THURSDAY

"Sadness is a natural thing Moli...when it arrives,
feel the ground as you sit comfortably.
Close your eyes and breathe long breaths like you
used to sit with your grandpa. " Tubee consoled
his friend. Soon enough sadness went by.

KID
FRIENDLY
HAPPY
HURT
INSPIRED
FEARFUL
AFRAID
EMPTY
CALM
GLAD !!!
SAD
HURT
FREE
STRONG
HAPPY
CALM
CREATIVE
FOCUSED
GRATEFUL
KIND
GLAD
HAPPY
TENDER
BRAVE
HAPPY
LOVING

Day to day Moli noticed the changing of
things and his feelings that came and went.
He saw no point in taking things to heart,
knowing how temporary everything was.

As Moli changed, things began to slowly change too.
Everyone enjoys being with the new happy and easy going Moli.
"Thank you Tubee for helping me see the changes!"
" Thank you grandpa for showing me how to
be the first person to love myself."

Jayada S. Sarela (Writer/Artist)

🌐 www.jayadasarela.com

📷 jayadasarela

She creates work that inspires others to connect with themselves, each other, and the world around them. She likes exploring cultures and nature and believes that we can learn from children just as they learn from us.

She is a children's and young adult book illustrator based in Germany. Inspired by her childhood, children, nature, magical moments, sea and fairytales. If she doesn't draw (rarely), she enjoys spending time with her family, tries to teach her dog to speak, travels, collects picture books and old magical things, cooks, reads and dreams about the house by the sea.

Marina Halak (Illustrator)

🌐 www.grosseaugenart.com

📷 grosseaugenart_illustration